THE LAW ON ARMED ROBBERY, THEFT AND HOUSE BREAKING IN
NIGERIA

THE LAW ON ARMED ROBBERY, THEFT AND HOUSE BREAKING IN
NIGERIA

A SURVEY OF ADAMAWA, BORNO, TARABA AND YOBE STATES.

Ishaku Gwangndi
& Sule Musa Tagi

authorHOUSE®

AuthorHouse™
1663 Liberty Drive
Bloomington, IN 47403
www.authorhouse.com
Phone: 1-800-839-8640

Published by AuthorHouse   07/21/2012

ISBN: 978-1-4772-1806-8 (sc)
ISBN: 978-1-4772-1807-5 (e)

DEDICATION

Dedicated to our families

PREFACE

The approach of the law to acts which interfere with the smooth running of the society is to prohibit such acts and in addition impose a penalty for breach of such prohibition. The object is to protect the society, individuals and their properties.

The offences of armed robbery, theft and house breaking are offences against the property. The provisions of the Penal Code Law relating to these offences are meant to provide protection for persons against interference with their properties.

The rate of commission of such offences has over the years been on the increase.

We have attempted in this work to provide some basic explanation of the reasons for this growth and indeed the reasons why the offences are committed. Thus paving the way for a discussion of the relevance and the statistics of the selected offences in Adamawa, Borno, Taraba and Yobe States.

It is obvious that significant number of allegations of the commission of such offences go unreported. The explanation for this may be found in a number of factors. One such factor is arrest. An appreciation of the law relating to arrest in this regard becomes necessary. We have been able to highlight the significance of criminal statistics against the back drop of the statistics of the offences of armed robbery, theft and house breaking. The revelation by available records shows a gap between the perception of the public with regards to the prevalence of these crimes and the reality in the records.

This it is hoped would be of immense benefit to law enforcement agents, criminologists, law lecturers, students of law and the general public.

FOREWORD

The Law on Armed Robbery, Theft and House breaking in Nigeria: a survey of Adamawa, Borno, Taraba and Yobe States presents the first comprehensive material on the area in practical terms where the law relating to the offences were highlighted and the statistics of the rate of the commission of the crimes brought out.

This, I believe, would not only be introducing a unique literature to the law library but will also go a long way in providing for those involved in the administration of criminal justice in the four states and indeed beyond a guide towards adopting the best strategy for tackling these crimes.

I commend the authors of the book for trying to lay the first foundation by advocating recourse to statistical records in the administration of criminal justice.

Mohammed Monguno,

Attorney-General and Commissioner for justice, Borno State.

ACKNOWLEDGEMENTS

A work of this nature necessarily brings together a number of people. We have not attempted to recognise all but our gratitude goes to all that in one way or the other contributed towards the success of this work.

First we thank Mal. Y.A. Muhammad, Ag. Dean of Law and Head of Department, Public Law for his encouragement and support.

The four Police Commands; Adamawa, Borno, Taraba and Yobe states who provided us with the most important data for this work. Mr. Yusuf Buba and Al-Yunus Musa for their kind assistance in collecting the data from the various police commands.

Mr. Nicholas P. Dibal, an author on statistics for taking his time to put in the statistical aspect of the work. Our special thanks go to

Alhaji Aminu Ayuba, Head of Department, Business Management, University of Maiduguri, for his untiring effort and assistance.

We also thank all members of the Faculty of law for their sense of cooperation.

We wish to acknowledge Professor Emmanuel M.K. Dawha of the Department of Library Science, University of Maiduguri Nigeria, who produced the author/subject index for this work.

Dr. Maryam Ishaku Gwangndi

Sule Musa Tagi

TABLE OF CASES

PAGE

Adeyemi v The State (1991)

1 NWLR (pt 170) 679   30

Ajao v State (unreported) S.C 75/1983   25

Alasho anaho and anor v Keffi N.A (1966)

NNLR37   39

Anderson v Wish (1980) Cr. App. Rep. 23   36

Audu Pankshin v Jos N.A (1962) NNCN 33   37

Babalola and anor v The State (1970)

All. NLR 44   29

Bozin v The State (1985)2 NWLR (pt 8) 465   26

Clark v State (9186) 4 NWLR (pt. 35) 381   38

Dennis James v Commisioner of Police

(1975) NNLR 37   37

Gambo dan Mamman v Zaria Native Authority

(1967) NNLR 1   49

Ikemson v State (1989) 3 NWLR (pt 110) 455   25

Mancini v D.P.P (1942) A.C 1   27

Martins v The State (1997) NWLR   26

(pt 481) 355

Maye Rukuba v Commisioner of Police

(1967) NNLR 114   41

Miller v Minister of Pensions (1947)

2 All. E.R. 372   27

Njuguma v R (1965) E.A 583   24

Nwomukoro and ors v The State (1995)

1 NWLR (pt 372) 432   28

Okobi v State (unreported) S.C 85/1983   30

Otti v State (1993) 4 NWLR (pt.290) 675   25

R v Desmond (1965) A.C 966   28

R v Fallow The Times Report of May 7th 1963   30

R v Hall (1849) 2. C. & K. 942   28

R v Lawrence (1932) 11 NLR 6   27

R v Lawrence (1971) 1 Q.B. 373   36

R v Taylor (1911) 1 K.B 674   36

R v Apesi (1961) WNLR 125   48

R v Bekun (1941) 7 WACA 45   24

R v Morris (1984) A.C 320   36

Royakiga v Tiv N. A. (1965) NMLR 402   37

State v Onwemunlo (1967—68) WSNLR 137   47

Uko v The State 1972 NSCC vol. 7600   50

Woolmington v D.P.P. (1935) A.C 462   27

TABLE OF STATUTES

The Constitution of the Federal Republic of Nigeria 1999

Section 37   5

Section 38   5

Section 39   5

Section 40   5

Section 41   5

Section 45(1)   5

Universal Declaration of Human Rights

Article 1   2

Article 30   4

The Penal Code Law Cap 89 Laws of Northern Nigeria 1963

Section 16   38

Section 286(1)(2)   33,34,35,38,39

Section 287   39

Section 288(1)   40

Section 290   42

Section 296(1)(2)(3)   23

Section 298   31

Section 299   32

Section 303(1)   32

Section 343   41,48,49,50

Section 346   44,46

Section 347   46

Section 353   51

Section 355   51

Section 356   49,52

Evidence Act Cap 112 Laws of the Federation of Nigeria 1990

Section 138(1)   26

Criminal Code Act Cap 385 Laws of thee Federation of Nigeria 1990   38,50

The Penal Code (Amendment) Edict No. 4 1975   37

The Penal Code (Amendment) Edict No. 5 1969   40

Robbery And Firearms (Special Provisions)

Decree No. 5   31

Tribunals (Certain Consequential Amendments Etc)

Decree No.62 1999

Robbery And Firearms Act No.47 1970

ABBREVIATION

A.C: Appeal Cases.

ALL E.R: All England Reports.

BSNLR: Borno State of Nigeria Law Reports.

C. & K: Carrington and Kirwan's Report

                (1843-1850)

E.A: East Africa.

NLR: Nigerian Law Reports.

NMLR: Nigerian Monthly Law Reports.

NNCN :   Northern Nigeria Cases Notes.

NNLR: Northern Nigeria Law Reports.

NRLR: Northern Region of Nigeria Law Reports.

NSCC: Nigeria Supreme Court Cases.

NWLR :   Nigeria Weekly Law Reports.

WACA: West African Court of Appeal.

WNLR: Western States of Nigeria Law Reports.

TABLE OF CONTENTS

Preface vii

Foreword ix

Acknowledgements xi

Table of Cases xiii

Table of Statutes xvii

Abbreviation xxi

Chapter I

Crime and Criminal Statistics 1

Introduction 1

The Relevance of Criminal Statistics 5

What is Crime 9

Causes of Crime 15

Social and Environmental (Economic) Factors 16

Unemployment. 18

Cross-Border Rebel Incursion 20

Chapter II

Armed Robbery 22

Definition of Armed Robbery 22

Proof Requirements For The Offence Of Robbery 26

Punishment For The Offence Of Armed Robbery 31

Chapter III

Theft. 33

Definition. 33

Mens Rea In Theft 38

Punishment For The Offence Of Theft. 39

Chapter IV

House Breaking 43

Burglary And House Breaking Distinguished 43

Ingredients For The Offence Of House Breaking 46

Entry. 48

Punishment for House Breaking .51

Chapter V

Major Crime Statistics In Adamawa, Borno, Taraba

And Yobe States 53

    Adamawa State. 55

    Borno State 56

    Yobe State. 57

    Taraba State 57

Appendices. 59

    Appendix I 59

    Appendix II 60

    Appendix III. 61

    Appendix IV. 62

Biblography 63

Index 69

CHAPTER I
Crime and Criminal Statistics

INTRODUCTION

The security of a nation should not be negotiable. Every government, regardless of its political ideology, has an inherent duty to ensure the safety of every life and property within its territory and jurisdiction. To this end, there must be ways and means of checking and controlling both internal and external elements and factors that could endanger and disrupt the national as well as individual welfare. In this regard therefore protective laws of some form become indispensable.

Chapter IV of the Constitution of the Federal Republic of Nigeria 1999, guarantees virtually every form of fundamental human right known to the Nigerian society. In addition, Nigeria is a member state of the Organisation of African Unity, ECOWAS and the United Nations. She is therefore bound by international conventions amongst nations eg the Universal Declaration of Human Rights adopted by the General Assembly of the United Nations on December 10, 1948.

The next most important duty any nation has is to ensure the basic human rights and freedom of the members of the society within its international boundaries. These include the right to life and property, human dignity and liberty, fair hearing, freedom of thought, conscience and religion, freedom of expression and the press, right to assembly and association, movement, non-discrimination and privacy[1].

Article 1 of the Universal Declaration of Human rights declares:

> All human beings are born free and equal in dignity and rights. They are endowed with reason and conscience and should act towards one another in a spirit of brotherhood.[2]

---

[1] See Sections 33-44 of the 1999 Constitution of the Federal Republic of Nigeria.

[2] See Final authorised text, issued by United Nations office of Public Information (Reprinted in UN, New York—DPI/15-3-37904, December

Fundamental human rights can only be meaningful when there is reciprocity of the rights with duties by members of the society. Absolute freedom according to Dr. A.O.P. Okumu is synonymous with anarchy. The absence of "acting towards one another in a spirit of brotherhood" is terrorism whether at national or International level.[3]

In the G.R.A. in Maiduguri today, some residents are barricaded like maximum security jail houses because of the most dangerous criminal elements of our society. And yet the people who live in those barricaded houses are some of the most harmless members of the society, e.g. University Lecturers, Judges, civil servants etc. The barricades are evidence of the fact that there are members of the Nigerian society who strongly believe that they are free to take away the lives and properties belonging to others in the dead of the night by using dangerous weapons as even when their victims are neither armed nor resistant. The rest of us are today being held at ransom by small but highly dangerous and destructive members of the society. No life, no property, no place in the present day Nigerian society can be said to be either safe or secure. Even those of us who know

---

1982).

[3] See the full text of a lecture delivered by Dr. O.A.P. Okumu at the University of Maiduguri on the occasion of the opening of the Accountancy Week on 12th May, 1986 at p. 20. Titled: The Necessity of Law in Society.

Chapter IV of the Nigerian Constitution in detail and are consulted on the Universal Declaration of Human Rights as adopted by the United Nations, live in fear for our lives and properties as if these sacred enactments have been abrogated[4].

The offences of Armed Robbery, Theft, house breaking and Burglary are punishable severely under Nigerian Laws and in particular the Penal Code. In spite of the penalties provided by Law for those offences the rate of the commission of these offences in the states under consideration continue to rise to a high degree which leaves us in an utmost helpless position.

Article 30 of the Universal Declaration of Human Rights declares:

> Nothing in this declaration may be interpreted as implying for any state, group or person any right to engage in any activity or to perform any act aimed at the destruction of any of the rights and freedoms set forth herein.[5]

---

[4]   Ibid.

[5]   Ibid.

Restriction on and derogation from fundamental rights is dealt with under Section 45(1) of the constitution of the Federal Republic of Nigeria 1999.

> Nothing in sections 37, 38, 39, 40, and 41 of this constitution shall invalidate any law that is reasonably justifiable in a democratic society—(a) in the interest of defence, public safety, public order, public morality or public health; or (b) for the purpose of protecting the rights and freedom of other persons.

Consequently, a law or regulation enacted by a Nigerian Government whether Federal or State is intended for the protection of the society, including rights to life, property and other freedoms is neither unconstitutional nor against the Universal Declaration of Human Rights.

THE RELEVANCE OF CRIMINAL STATISTICS

The role the police plays is of vital importance in this regard. Can such records be taken as the actual crimes recorded for these periods? The problems faced by various agencies vested with the recording of crime are not peculiar to Nigeria alone. Hence it is important therefore to look at these problems and see ways of improving crime recording and also to proffer solutions. Hence the meaning of criminal statistics has to be explored and explained effectively for the purpose of understanding and appreciating the problems. In this regard the role the police plays in the recording of crime statistics annually is of utmost importance and significance. Perhaps it is because the police are actively involved in keeping the records that is why it is intended through this work to appeal to legislators and administrators to look into the affairs of the police in Nigeria so as to improve on keeping proper records. In consequence, laws and other things that need to be put in place should be done with a sense of seriousness and clear vision for the future generations of this great country. In this regard Mr. Figbene Membere, a senior police officer in the Nigerian Police Force, had this to say in his manual for the police.

> Crime statistics are a collection of crime data or facts expressed in figures and signs showing at a glance the totality of crime situation or state of crime in any given area. The information is collected in respect of total number of cases reported, number of cases accepted as true cases, number of cases refused, number of cases prosecuted, convicted or discharged.

Summary of important cases reported usually issued monthly, shows offences prevalent month by month in any particular area.[6]

The significance of the annual reports on criminal statistics is that it shows the nature and extent of the crime problem just as Geoffrey Millerson sees the annual reports on crime statistics as:

representing an attempt to measure the nature and extent of crime problems.[7]

Indeed this work has been carried out in the spirit of trying to find out the nature and extent of the problems, possible damages and dangers the offences of armed robbery, theft, burglary and house breaking have had on the security of lives and properties within the North East sub-region. It is common knowledge that armed robbery attacks are being unleashed on innocent citizens on high ways. People no longer feel safe to travel. These days people have organised themselves into

---

[6] C.F.L. Membere. Standard Police Manual Vol. 1 Police (Nigeria) and Law Enforcement. (Benin City: P. Koda pubs. Ltd 1982) p. 164 cited in N. Aduba; "Recording of Crime in Nigeria: Problems and Prospects" *Journal of Contemporary Legal Problems*(1992) Jus. Vol.3 Nos 7 & 8 p.2.

[7] Geoffrey Millerson "Criminal Statistics and the Perks Committee (1968) Crime. L. R. p.478."

vigilante groups in a bid to safeguard their lives and properties. People now sleep with only one eye closed because of thieves, burglars and housebreakers. These have in consequence resulted in both communal and personal economic losses to the benefit of these men of the underworld.

> It has also been noted that criminal statistics is of value to legislators and administrators who intend to counteract criminality because of its utility in the measurement of trends of criminality.[8]

It was also observed that criminality statistics may have research value to scholars from various fields depending on what particular item of information about offences and offenders have been tabulated and from what type of records these items have been drawn. It was expected that the student of penal treatment might hope to learn from them something about recidivism, for instance, and the students of judicial or police administration something concerning the sentencing practices of the courts and the manner in which the prosecutor and the police deal with the accused or the suspect. It was equally thought that those interested in the rising problems of the

---

[8]   Professor Thorsten Sellin; "The Significance of Records of Crimes", *The Law Quarterly Review,* (1991) P.489 at pp.491-492.

causation of crime would naturally hope to find useful research data in criminal statistics.[9]

WHAT IS CRIME

There is always difficulty in giving or providing a universal definition of crime. The reason is very simple. The fact is that acts defined as criminal vary with time and space. An act may be a crime in one society but not in another. Likewise, an act defined as a crime at any time may not be at another. In some cases even if same or similar acts are defined as crimes in different societies, the gravity or seriousness to which each society views the act may be different.[10]

In addition to the reason given above, there are also conflicting views on the definition of crime among journalists and social scientists, mostly bordering on ethical and ideological orientation. On the definition of crime, a United Nations Research Institute observed:

> Crime in the sense of breach of legal prohibition is
> a universal concept, but what actually constitutes a

---

[9]   Ibid at pp. 491-492.

[10]   A.B. Dambazau: Criminology and Criminal Justice (Nigerian Defence Academy Kaduna 1999 at p.32).

crime and how seriously it should be regarded, varies enormously from one society to another. Perceptions of crime are not determined by any objective indicator of the degree of injury or damage but by cultural values and power relations[11].

In a strict legal definition, however, a crime is a violation of the criminal law, which is subsequently followed by a legal punishment. In criminal law a crime is an act or omission, which attracts sanctions, such as fine, imprisonment or even execution[11a]. A crime in law consists of two basic elements, the *actus reus* and the *mens rea*. The *actus reus* is the physical element or the guilty act, and it requires proof. Where there is no actus reus, there is no crime. It includes all the elements in the definition of crime, with the exception of the mental element[12]. The actus reus could be made up of conduct, its consequences and the circumstances in which the conduct takes place[13]. The second element, *mens rea* is the mental element or guilty mind. It is basically the intention, and a man is said

---

[11]   State in Disarray: The Social Effects of Globalisation, UN Research Institute for Social Development, 1995.

[11a] As put by Conklin "Crime is behavior that is subject to legally defined punishment" in Conklin J.E., Criminology 3rd ed.(New York: Macmilian Publishing Company, New York 1986) p.6.

[12]   Smith, J.C. and B. Hogan, Criminal Law, (London; Butterworths, 1988).

[13]   Ibid p.35.

to intend doing something if he foresaw and desired it. The desire for the consequences is the basic factor of intention. Mens rea is not required for all crimes. There is no singular definition of mens rea because every crime has its own mens rea. To demonstrate *mens rea* it must be proven that an individual intentionally, knowingly, recklessly, or negligently behaves in a given manner or caused a given result. Crime can be dichotomised into serious and minor, felony and misdemeanour; *mala in se* and *mala prohibitum*[14]. Crimes can also be against persons and property; and so on.

This work is centred on crimes that go against the person as well as the property of the person. We have also touched on the concern of criminologist because they are very much concerned with all potentially criminal behaviour, not only in the strict legal sense. The definition of crime among criminologists has therefore recognised factors such as value systems, norms and religious attitudes in a given culture[15].

While the classical school emphasised the legal definition of crime, the positive school defined crime in the context of disease. Positivist

---

[14]   Mala in se Crimes are those which are almost virtually accepted as wrong or bad in themselves, such as assault and rape. Mala prohibitum are those which are statutory in nature, and may pass in and out of the criminal law.

[15]   A.B. Dambazau op. cit.; page

rejected the legal definition of crime because according to them, the concept of crime cannot be accepted as a legal category "since the factors which produce the legal definition are contingent and capricious[16]"

Durkhein defined crime within a social context. He saw crime as a social product determined by social conditions, capable of being controlled only in social terms, crime is therefore normal in all societies according to him, and that "a society exempt from crime would necessitates standardised of moral concepts of all individuals which is neither possible nor desirable"[17]. In the final analysis, Durkhein defined crime as "an act which offends strong and defined state of collective conscience[18]. This is basically the functionist or consensus view, which the society functioning as an integrated, stable structure because of agreement or consensus among its members on certain rules and values recognised and respected by all[19].

---

[16] Jeffrey, C.R, "An integrated Theory of Crime and Criminal Behaviour" *Journal of Criminology and Police Science*. 49 (1959) pp.533-555.

[17] Durheim, E, The Division of Labour in Society, G. Sinpdon (trans) (New York: Mc Millian, 1933).

[18] Ibid.

[19] See Shepherd, J. Sociology, (St. Paul, Min, West publishing, 1981).

The Nigerian society has a legal system which has rules and regulations agreed upon to be respected by all members of the society and any violation attracts sanctions. The legal system is therefore a reflection of this consensus. A crime is therefore a violation of the rules agreed to be respected by all members of the society, and upon which rest members of the society mete sanctions upon those guilty of the violation. It is for the same reason that the legal system views crime as a public wrong because

> crimes . . . are wrong which the judges have held, or parliament has from time to time laid down, are sufficiently

> injurious to the public to warrant the application of criminal procedure to deal with them[20]". Likewise, it is moral wrong because according to Lord Devlin, there is a public morality which is an essential part of the bondage which keeps society together; and that society may use the criminal law to preserve morality

---

[20]   Smith and Hogan, op. cit. p.19.

in the same way that it uses it to preserve anything else that is essential to its existence[21].

Criminal law is therefore seen to be concerned with public wrongs or wrongs against the society. Such wrongs involve acts of physical violence, such as murder and rape, infringement of property rights such as theft, fraud and burglary . . . and so on[22]. It is therefore of utmost importance that murder may be a consequence of armed robbery, theft, housebreaking or burglary. Allen sums it with the following observation:

Crime is crime because it consist in wrong doing which directly and in serious degree threatens the security or well being of society, and because it is not safe to leave to redressable only by compensation of the party injured[23].

---

[21] Lord Delvin, "The end of Morals" *The Maccabean Lecture*, 45, proc. of British Academy, 1959, p 129.

[22] A.B. Danbazau op. cit.,.

[23] Allen, C.K. "The Nature of Crime", *Journal of Comparative Legislation,* (1931).

CAUSES OF CRIME

Criminal behaviour may not be unconnected to some prevailing factors in the society. We are of the view that the periods under consideration have seen a downturn in the economic life of the Nigerian society. The hard economic life has resulted into many anti-social behaviours that are criminal on the part of some individuals. As a result innocent citizens are made victims of these criminal tendencies. In this regard, any attempt to find fixed causal patterns of criminal behaviour is usually difficult because of the interplay of so many factors which may differ not only from one individual to another, but also from one society to another. Researchers have shown that the causes of crime are multiple and could be traced to biogenetic factors, such as genetic mutation and heredity[24]. Psychological factors include

---

[24]   Hooton, E, The American Criminal, (Cambridge Mass: Harvard University Press: 1939); L.Taylor, Born to Crime: The Genetic Causes of Criminal Behaviour, London. Greenwood press, 1984).

issues, such as personality disorders[25] and sociological factors, such as learning and the environment[26].

SOCIAL AND ENVIRONMENTAL (ECONOMIC) FACTORS

The environment is said to play a significant role in determining criminal behaviour of both the juvenile and adult offender. Factors within the environment considered to be crucial in contributing to criminal behaviour include urbanisation, poverty, unemployment, corruption, poor education, high technology, drug abuse, architectural or environmental designs etc. Most relevant for consideration by the Nigerian society is the observation made by a member of the European parliament for South West London, Anita Pollock, while agreeing that those who commit crimes deserve to be punished. She observed that:

---

[25]   D.Abramen. Crime and the Human Mind, (New York: Columbia University Press, 1994); J.Bowlby "Forty-four Juvenile Thieves", *International Journal of Psychoanalysis*, (1944) 25; 1-57; S. Glueck and E. Glueck. Unravelling Juvenile Delinquency. (New York: Harper & Row 1950); B.F. Skinner, The Behaviour of Organisms, (New York, 1938), J. Piaget, The Moral Judgement of the Child, (London 1932).

[26]   Sutherland, E.H. Principles of Criminology, (Philadelphia: 1947); Lippincott; E.Durkheim.

. . . we need to recognise that there are links between social conditions and crime and understanding these links are what we should be about. Tackling crimes and the environment in which crime flourishes are alternatives, they need to be considered together. Inner city decay and drug abuse, child poverty, cuts in the youth service and failures in the education system are all issues to be addressed . . . Lack of training opportunities as well as unemployment, and the widening inequalities between rich and poor . . . the relationship between unemployment, poverty, urban degradation and crime is very apparent[27].

"Poverty", according to Clark, "is the mother of crime"[28]. It is our humble submission that there is a direct relationship between economic and social stress and criminal act. Inequality is said to affect social relationships especially in a situation in which while the

---

[27] This observation was made during a meeting between London members of the European Parliament and Sir Paul Condon and his team at New Scotland Yard in 1998 (Downloaded from the internet) See A.B. Dambazau op. cit. p. 77.

[28] Clark R. Crime in America (New York: Simon & Schuster, 1970).

income of the rich rises, the poor feel relatively more deprived. Such deprivation, it is argued can lead to activation and subsequently[29].

UNEMPLOYMENT

Closely related to poverty is unemployment. Unemployment has been defined as "enforced idleness of wage earners that are able and willing to work but cannot find jobs"[30]. It has been argued that unemployment can lead to crime as a result of feeling of deprivation, rejection and personal failure. It is also claimed that unemployment could lead to mental stress, apathy and illness, factors that could pave way to criminal behaviour[31].

Does unemployment on its own cause crime? Are there intervening factors to further explain the incidence of crime even in periods of high unemployment? It is not also true that many of the employed commit crimes? Certainly unemployment creates the environment in which frustration breeds, stress increases, resulting in a feeling of hopelessness, especially in a society where there is no

---

[29] See Susan E. Mayer, "The Consequences of Inequality: The State of Current Research" *Joint Centre for Poverty Research News*, Vol. No. 3 (Summer 1998).

[30] See Dermot Walse and Poola, A Dictionary of Criminology. P.227.

[31] A.B. Dambazau, op. cit; p.78

provision for social welfare in order to give temporary relief for the unemployed. This situation itself becomes an instigator for criminal behaviour[32].

It is our submission that unemployment has a direct link to poverty. To this end the Nigerian government which Borno, Adamawa, Yobe and Taraba states are parts of must do something urgently to address the issue of poverty by providing job opportunities and also by embarking on programme of self reliance to its citizens. These will go a long way in checking the rate of the commission of the crimes of armed robbery, theft, burglary and housebreaking in the society. These crimes have a direct connection with lack of economic empowerment of the people. The Federal Government's current programme for poverty alleviation should be handled with all seriousness of purpose. The programme should be implemented in such a way that its effect is felt among those it is meant to address. Until these crimes, particularly that of armed robbery, are reduced to the barest minimum the entire members of the society shall know no peace. The constitutional rights that guarantee security of lives and properties will remain only on the pages of the books if these criminal tendencies are not checked. These can only be done by providing the

---

[32]   Ibid. p. 79.

society with meaningful social and economic condition in order for the citizen to lead a meaningful life by alleviating sufferings and eradicating abject neglect.

When a man is hungry, he is an angry man and he is bound to react by taking revenge even on those who are not the direct cause of his pathetic situation. Frustration to some certain extent is borne out of abject poverty, degradation and total neglect.

CROSS-BORDER REBEL INCURSION

For most of these states they share boundaries with other countries where war has caused a significant movement of the people, some dangerously armed. These rebels engage in armed robbery to acquire means of prosecuting their cause. Invariably reports have it time and time again that some of the armed robbers arrested are of foreign nationalities. The inability to police our borders effectively has given opportunity for cross-border raids by armed men who after committing acts of robbery flee back to their nations. Of course various efforts are being made to tackle such situations by various nations through international protocol. The efficacy of these steps however remains doubtful as those that engage in such activities are not controlled by their governments, indeed rebels.

The police play a vital role in the criminal justice system. The police should as a matter of priority be well funded, equipped in order to face the challenges of their duties. In fact without the police apprehending offenders and reporting the same, the true position of the rate of the commission of all crimes will not be made available and even where they are reported, the question is, how many are actually reported? In a situation where the armed bandits, local thieves, burglars and housebreakers, are more equipped with arms, what can a defenceless policeman do? Even where an incidence of crime is being committed, and a report is made, the police in some cases would have no option than to pretend that they didn't get such a report requiring urgent attention.

CHAPTER II

Armed Robbery

DEFINITION OF ARMED ROBBERY

Black's Law Dictionary[1] defined the term Armed Robbery as:

> An aggravated form of robbery in which the defendant is armed with dangerous weapon, though it is not necessary to prove that he used the weapon to effectuate the robbery. The taking of property from person or in presence of another by use of force or threatening use of force while armed with a dangerous weapon.

---

[1] 5th Edition at p. 99.

The same dictionary[2] defined robbery as:

> Felonious taking of money, personal property, or any other article of value, in the possession of another from his person or immediate presence and against his will accompanied by means of force or fear.

Robbery is defined by the section 296 of the Penal Code[3]. The section provides as follows:

S. 296(1)—In all robbery there is theft or extortion.

S. 296(2)—Provides the condition under which theft is robbery.

> Theft is robbery if, in order to commit the theft or in committing the theft or in carrying away or attempting to carry away property obtained by the theft, the offender for that end voluntarily causes or attempts to cause to any person death or hurt or wrongful restraint or fear of instant death or of instant hurt or of wrongful restraint.

---

2   p.119.

3   Cap.89 Laws of Northern Nigeria.

While S.296(3) provides that:

> Extortion is robbery, if the offender at the time
> of committing the extortion is in the presence of
> the person put in fear and commits the extortion
> by putting that person in fear of instant wrongful
> restraint to that person or to some other person and
> by so putting in fear induces the person so put in fear
> then and there to deliver up the thing extorted.

The essence of robbery is theft. In all robbery cases there must be either theft or extortion and there must be attempt or threat of death or hurt of grievous nature too the person or victim. The offence of robbery is not restricted to theft or extortion by use of force but it also includes a situation where there is fraudulent conversion by use of force. The force or threat of force, if it is to amount to robbery must be used in order that the accused person might steal. In *R v Bekun*[4] where A and his companion deposited valuable property in B's house and then went out to buy some meat and were attacked and killed on the way by B who intended to, and did in fact steal the property. It was held that this is robbery. But in an East African case

---

[4]   (1941) 7 W.A.C.A p.45.

of *Njuguma v R*[5] the accused having burgled a house and stole some item therein was discovered without a chase at a distance of about five hundred yards away where he resisted the complainant (owner), it was held that the offence was not robbery but burglary and theft because the element of using violence immediately after the act was lacking. As Richard concluded

> It is clear that there is no robbery if the force is used
>
> or threatened after the time of theft.[6]

In *Ikemson v State*[7] the court held that the offence of robbery with firearms is committed where, at the time of commission of robbery, the accused is proved to have been armed with 'firearm' or 'offensive weapon' within the meaning of section 9 of the Firearms (Special Provision) Act No.47 of 1970. Any person in company of a person so armed, or aiding or abetting the commission of the offence is similarly guilty[8].

---

[5] (1965) E.A. 583

[6] Richard C. Criminal Law 12th ed., (London Butterworth 1992) p.20. See also Otti v State (1993) 4 NWLR (pt.290) 675.

[7] See also Ajao v State (unreported) S.C. 75/1983 in Digest of the Supreme Court Cases 1956-84 Vol. 10 394.

[8] (1989) 3 NWLR (PT.110) 455.

PROOF REQUIREMENTS FOR THE
OFFENCE OF ROBBERY

For the prosecution to secure convictions on whom the burden of proof lies, for the offence of robbery the Court of Appeal in the case of *Martins v The State*[9] held dismissing the appeal that it has to prove beyond reasonable doubt the following ingredients.

a) That there was robbery.

b) That the robbery was an armed robbery; and

c) That the accused was the robber.

A conviction for the offence of armed robbery can only be sustained where the above mentioned ingredients of the offence are proved beyond reasonable doubt. If the prosecution fails to prove any of these ingredients, then it has not proved its case beyond reasonable doubt. In such a case, the accused is entitled to an acquittal[10].

---

[9]   (1997) 1 N.W.L.R (pt. 110) 455.

[10]   See Bozin v The State (1985) 2 NWLR (pt 8) p. 465 See also Ikemson v State (1989) 3 NWLR (pt. 110) 455.

In criminal cases the legal burden of proof is always on the prosecution. The standard of proof required for the discharge of that burden is that the prosecution has to prove the guilt of the accused beyond reasonable doubt. The standard is imported by section 138(1) of the Evidence Act[11] which stipulates that:

> If the commission of a crime by a party to any proceeding is directly in issue in any proceeding civil or criminal, it must be proved beyond reasonable doubt.

The requirement that the guilt of the accused has to be proved beyond reasonable doubt was imported from the English Common Law and has been re-affirmed by the House of Lords in such cases as *Woolmington v D.P.P.*[12], *Mancini v D.P.P*[13] and the Privy Council on appeal in the Nigerian case of *R v Lawrence*[14].

The term reasonable doubt is not capable of precise definition although its connotation is readily conceived. It does not mean proof

---

[11]   Cap. 112 Laws of the Federation of Nigeria 1990.

[12]   (1935) A.C. 462.

[13]   (1942) A.C.1.

[14]   (1932) 11 N.L.R. p.6 at p.7.

beyond all doubt. Commenting on its nature Denning J. (as he then was) said in *Miller v Minister of Pensions*[15].

> It need not reach certainty, but must carry a high degree of probability. Proof beyond reasonable doubt does not mean proof beyond the shadow of doubt.

Originally in England actual violence was necessary for robbery but this was changed and any thereat_of violence as a result of which goods were taken, is now enough to amount to armed robbery, as was shown by Lord Moris of Borth—Y—GEST in *R v Hall, R v Desmond*[16] where he said:

> There is little doubt that the writings and the decisions in regard to robbery reveal a continuous and progressive process of definition. In earlier times the offence was probably limited to cases where there was actual violence to the person and a forcible taking from the person. Gradually the conceptions as what constituted robbery were extended. Actual violence was not necessary. There might be a putting in fear of

---

[15]   (1947) 2 All. E.R. 372.

[16]   (1965) A.C. 966 at p. 979

violence by a threat of violence. That could be called constructive violence.

In *Nwomukoro and ORS v The State*[17]

Acholono, JCA aptly stated the position thus:

> For an act to constitute robbery, there must be that experience by the victim of fear and intimidation brought about by apprehension of possible violence to his person before the robbery. The fear of possible injury instilled on the victim must of necessity precede the taking. I believe that intimidation of constructive force by which what is commonly described as fear of God is put in a person and in which a crime of robbery is committed shall include all administration of force or menace and other means by which the victim is put in fear sufficient to sustain at the material time free exercise of his will power as to make it awfully difficult or near possible for him to offer any resistance to any one taking his property.

---

[17] (1995) 1 NWLR (part 372) p. 432 at 449.

The test as to what amounts to a threat of violence was considered in the case of *Babalola and Anor v The State*[18] where the court held that if a person threatens another with a gun the natural inference is that the threatened person would expect to receive actual violence if he did not accede to the order to hand over his money. He could not, be expected to ask the person threatening him to show him whether the gun was loaded or not so as to determine whether he was put in fear of actual violence. The test is whether the threatened person reasonably believes in the apparent circumstances that the threat is likely to be carried out and being spout in fear hands over his money (or the goods demanded).

Where several persons went out to steal and unknown to them one of them used violence in the course of stealing the rest of the members of the group are only guilty of stealing and not robbery unless it can be established that they were parties to the use of violence by the other members. This is the decision in the English case of *R v Fallow*[19]. This proposition has no stand in our judicial circle where the Supreme Court refused to follow this decision in the case of *Adeyemi v The State*[20].

---

[18]   (1970) 1 All. N.L.R at P.49

[19]   The Times Report of May, 7th 1963.

[20]   (1991) 1 N.W.L.R. (part 170) 679 See also Okobi v State (Unreported) SC/85/1983 in Digest of the Supreme Court Cases 1956-84 Vol. 10 394 where

PUNISHMENT FOR THE OFFENCE OF ARMED ROBBERY

The offence of robbery is punishable with imprisonment for 10 years with or without fine and canning. But if the offender is armed with a dangerous or offensive weapon or in company with one or more other person, he is liable to imprisonment for life, with or without canning[21]. Because of the alarming increase in cases of armed robbery after the civil war the Robbery and Firearms (Special Provision) Decree[22] was passed to provide severer punishment for the offence and a more speedy mode of trial. Under the Decree the offence of robbery was punishable with imprisonment for not less than 21 years. If the offender is armed with any firearm or any offensive weapon or is in company with any person so armed, or at or immediately before or immediately after the time of the robbery he wounds any person the punishment was death which was executed by hanging or by firing squad. This Decree was amended by subsequent Decrees, the most recent was Decree No.5 of 1984[23] hence giving exclusive jurisdiction for the trial of robbery and armed robbery cases to the Armed Robbery Tribunal. Recently

---

the court held that an accused cannot be convicted of robbery unless there is evidence of threat of actual violence used or threatened in order to retain the stolen property.

[21] See Section 298 of the Penal Code.

[22] Decree, No.47 of 1970.

[23] As amended by Robbery and Firearms (Special Provisions) Decree No. 21 of 1984

the Federal Government by Decree No.62 of 1999 abolished the Armed Robbery Tribunal and the Court having jurisdiction for the trial of the offence of robbery is the High Court of a State. Appeal from the decision of the High Court goes to the Court of Appeal and from the Court of Appeal to the Supreme Court.

Section 299 of the Penal Code makes any person who attempts to commit robbery punishable with imprisonment for a term of 14 years. And section 303 (1) (b) (iii) of the Penal Code provides that:

S. 303(1)—If at any time of committing or attempting to commit robbery

b) the offender:

iii) Uses or attempts or offers to use, or bears, any firearm or with anything resembling a firearm, the imprisonment with which such offender shall be punished shall not be less than life, with or without caring.

The term "firearm" is defined in section 303(3) of the Penal Code to mean any barrelled weapon of any description from which any shot, bullet or other missile can be discharged.

CHAPTER III

Theft

DEFINITION

Theft is defined as:

> The fraudulent taking of personal property belonging
> to another, from his possession or from the possession
> of some person holding the same for him, without his
> consent, with intent to deprive the owner of the value
> of the same, and to appropriate it to the use or benefit
> of the person taking.[1]

---

[1]   Black's Law Dictionary op. cit. p.1324.

The offence of theft is prescribed by the Penal Code in Section 286 as follows:

Section 286(1) provides:

> Whoever, intending to take dishonestly any movable property out of the possession of any person without that person's consent, moves that property in order to take it is said to commit theft.

Subsection (2) provides that:

> Whoever dishonestly abstracts, diverts consumes or uses any electricity or electric current is said to commit theft.

Under section 286 of the Penal Code, the *actus reus* of theft is moving in order to take out of someone's possession without consent. Thus, for a charge of theft to be sustained under section 286 of the Penal Code, the accused must have taken a thing capable of being stolen out of someone's possession without his consent. So if 'A' watches 'B' drop her wallet but instead of alerting her, decides to keep quiet until she disappears, his taking of the wallet and subsequent disposal of its content will not make him a thieve.

The 'taking' for it to amount to theft must not only be out of someone's possession but also without his consent[2]. Under section 286 of the Penal Code, the crucial period of lack of consent is at the time of the taking so that if a hirer of a bicycle later decides to sell it off to pocket the money, his subsequent fraudulent intention to convert the proceeds of the sale will not make him a thief under section 286 Penal Code. This will only amount to criminal misappropriation under section 308 of the Code.

The consent mentioned in the definition may be express or implied and may be given either by the person in possession or by any person having for that purpose the authority either express or implied.

For one to satisfy the other actus reus bit of section 286 of the Penal Code, the "taking" need not be complete. It suffices if the accused starts to move the property or causes it to move. For more elucidation, a person is said to cause a thing to move by removing an obstacle which prevented it from moving or by separating it from any other

---

[2]   cf. Smith J.C and Hogan B, Criminal Law, 17th ed. (London; Butherworths 1992). p.497.

thing as well as by actually moving it. So if A intending to steal a book from B's brief case begins to take out the book where upon B suddenly shouts at him and he drops it back into the brief case, A's conduct amounts to stealing and not merely an attempt to steal[3]. In *R v Morris*[4], D and E were convicted of theft. The accused persons had changed a lower price label for a higher price label on goods which they were about to purchase. D was arrested after he had paid the lower price at the check out while E was arrested before he had gone through the check out. E's counsel had submitted that E had not appropriated the goods merely by switching the price labels. The appeals both at the Court of Appeal and House of Lords failed the requirement of appropriation having been satisfied[5].

And in *R v Lawrence*[6], on arrival in London P, an Italian student spoke little English, showed a piece of paper to D, a taxi-driver on which was written an address. The address was not far away and the normal fare would have been about 50p., but D said it was a long way off and would be expensive. When P. Tendered a £1 note D said this would not be enough and from P's wallet, which P was holding open, he took a further £1 note and a £5 note. On appeal it

---

3   R v Taylor (1911) 1 K.B. 674.

4   (1984) A.C 320.

5   See also Anderson v Walsh Cr. App. Rep. 373.

6   (1971) 1 Q.B.373.

was argued that D had not stolen the money because P had consent to its being taken by D. It was held P's consent was no defence and appeal failed.

The 'taking' may not be conventionally understood as for instance, where one takes something by trick. In *Royakiga v Tiv N.A.*[7] it was held that taking by sleight of hand without either the knowledge or consent of the lawful possessor of the property is theft and not cheating, the word "taking", therefore, must not be understood as taking away the property.

For the prosecution to secure conviction for the offence of theft, it must prove that the thing 'taken' was in the possession (actual or constructive) of someone else. It must be shown that an act by way of adverse interference with or usurpation of an owner's right did occur. It cannot succeed in establishing this merely because the accused does not deny the prosecution's story. In Audu Pankshin v Jos N.A.[8] a Lower Court accepted the evidence that the property allegedly stolen belonged to Jos Native Authority on the basis that the accused did not deny that it was so. On appeal it was held that the Lower Court had erred in Law and its verdict was therefore set

---

[7]   (1962) N.M.L.R. 402.

[8]   (1962) N.N.C.N. 33

aside. In this case of Dennis James v C.O.P.[9] the appellant had access as a workman to a Teacher Training College. The chief Magistrate found that the microscope was stolen from the building used for the custody of the microscope and convicted him of aggravated theft under section 288(1) of the Penal Code. It was held that thmicroscope was in the laboratory for the purpose of experiments and teaching. It would not be correct to say that the laboratory was used for the custody of the microscope unless the microscope had been stored in the laboratory and the primary purpose of the laboratory was the custody of the microscope. Accordingly, the conviction of aggravated theft under section 288(1) Penal Code was set aside and a conviction under section 287 substituted[10].

MENS REA IN THEFT

The form of mental element required for purpose of theft under section 286 Penal Code is "dishonest intention". The word dishonest is defined in section 16 of the Penal Code.

---

[9]   (1975) N.N.L.R. 136.

[10]   See Clark v State (1986) 4 NWLR (pt. 35) 381 where the court is considering the requirements for proving stealing under the Criminal Code identified: a. fraudulent taking and b. that the goods stolen belong to some person other than the taker, as essential.

Section 16 of the Code provides that:

> A person is said to do a thing dishonestly who does
> that thing with the intention of causing a wrongful
> gain to himself or another or of causing a wrongful
> loss to any other person

The position of the law under the Penal Code is that theft is committed even though there is no intention to permanently deprive the owner of the property. So it was held in *Alasho Anaho and Anor v Keffi N.A.*[11] that the offence of theft in section 286 of the Penal Code may be committed even though there is no intention permanently to deprive the owner[12].

PUNISHMENT FOR THE OFFENCE OF THEFT

The punishment for the offence of theft is provided for under the Penal Code in sections 287 and 288 respectively, section 287(1) provides:

---

[11]   (1966) N.N.L.R. 37 at 38. See particularly pp. 42-43 of the report.

[12]   This is different from the position in England where the requirement in respect of mens rea of theft is "(1) dishonesty and (2) with the intention to permanently deprive the other" in Smith J.C and Hogan B., Criminal Law, 17th ed. London Butherworths 1992 p.536.

"Whoever commits theft shall be punished with imprisonment for a term which extends to five years."

Subsection (2) provides:

where:

a) The value of the property stolen is below the sum of =N= 100.00; and

b) The theft is not committed in any building or dwelling house, the punishment shall be twelve strokes of the cane for the first offence and a fine of fifty Naira for subsequent offences.

Section 288[13] of the Code provides:

Whoever commits theft in or from any building, tent or vessel, which building, tent or vessel is used as a human dwelling or used for the Custody of property, or in or from any railway carriage, lorry, omnibus or aircraft used for the conveyance of passengers or goods,

---

[13] The Section was substituted with another by the Penal Code Law (Amendment) Edict No.5 1969.

shall be punished with imprisonment for a term which may extend to seven year or with fine or with both.

In 1969 the Military Government of North Eastern State amended the section and substituted it with a new section. The new section increased the penalty for the offence to "not less than ten years and not less than twelve strokes of the cane, with or without fine."

The new subsection (2) provided:

> Whoever attempts to commit an offence under subsection (1) shall be punished with imprisonment for a term of not les than seven years and not less than twelve strokes of the cane, with or without fine.

And further defined a building in subsection (3) as follows:

> For the purpose of this section "building" means a structure of any kind whether permanent or temporary and includes a hut, store, granary, and a compound completely enclosed by a wall or other structure[14].

---

[14] See the case of Maye Rukuba v Commisioner of Police (1967) NNLR 114, where the court defined building as used in Section 343 of the Penal Code

Different specie of the offence of theft is provided for under section 289 of the code. The section provides.

> Whoever being a clerk or servant or being employed in the capacity of clerk or several, commits theft in respect of any property in the possession of his master or employer shall be punished with imprisonment for a term which may extend so seven years or with fine or with both.

It would be seen that while the maximum punishment provided for theft cases other than that set out in section 288, is five years with or without a fine the case of section 289 the fact relationship of an accused to the property is taken into consideration and severe penalty of seven years with or without a fine is provided[15].

Law.

[15] See also section 290 of the Code which made provision for a severer penalty where theft is committed after preparing to cause death, hurt or restraint in order to commit theft.

CHAPTER IV
House Breaking

BURGLARY AND HOUSE BREAKING DISTINGUISHED

The term Burglary has been defined as follows:

> the crime of burglary consisted of breaking and
> entering of a dwelling house of another in the
> nighttimes with the intent to commit a felony
> therein[1].

House breaking has been as:

---

[1]   Black's Law Dictionary op. cit. p.179

"Also "breaking" means the tearing away or removal of any part of a house or of the locks, latches, or other fastenings intended to secure it, or otherwise exerting force to gain an entrance, with criminal intent: or violently or forcibly breaking out of a house, after having unlawfully entered it, in an attempt to escape. Actual "breaking" involves application of some force, though the slightest force is sufficient, e.g. an actual "breaking" may be made by any covering or fastening of the premises, such as lifting a latch, drawing a bolt etc."[2]

Both the offence of burglary and house breaking have the same ingredients. The only dichotomy between the two offences is in respect of time of their commission. The Law draws a difference between the two offences particularly in terms of punishment. If the offence is committed in or during the day time it is called house breaking and is punishable with imprisonment for 14 years. If committed in the night it is called burglary and is punishable with imprisonment for life[3]. For the purpose of the law, the period of night starts from 6.30 p.m. to 6.30.a.m section 346 of the Penal Code defines House breaking as follows:

---

[2]   Ibid. p. 171.

[3]   See Sectons 354 and 357 of the Penal Code.

A person is said to commit house breaking who commits house trespass, if he effects his entrance into a house or any part of it in any of the six ways herein after described; or if being in the house or any part of it for the purpose of committing an offence or having committed an offence therein, he quits the house or any part of it in any of such ways, that is to say:

a) If he enters or quits through a passage made by himself or by any abettor of the house trespass in order to commit the house trespass;

b) If he enters or quits through any passage not intended by any person, other than himself or an abettor of the offence, for human entrance, or through any passage to which he has obtained access by scaling or climbing over any wall or building;

c) If he enters or quits through any passage which he or any abettor of the house trespass has opened in order to commit the house to trespass by any means by which that passage was not intended by the occupier of the house to be opened;

d) If he enters or quits by opening any lock in order to commit the house trespass or in order to quit the house after a house trespass;

e) If he effects his entrance or departure by using criminal force or committing an assault or by threatening any person with assault.

f) If he enters or quits by any passage which he knows to have been fastened against such entrance or departure and to have been unfastened by himself or by an abettor of the house trespass.

For the purpose of house breaking by night termed or called burglary, in other jurisdictions, section 347 of the Penal Code provides that:

> Whoever commits house breaking between sunset and sun rise, is said to commit house breaking by night.

The explanation given by the Penal Code in respect of the word house as used in section 346 of the Code is that: The word "house" in this section includes any place which maybe the subject of house trespass; while building was defined in section 283(3) of the Penal Code.

INGREDIENTS FOR THE OFFENCE

OF HOUSE BREAKING

Breaking: breaking is an essential ingredient of both burglary and house breaking. So if a man leaves the door of his dwelling house open and a thief enters through the same door the offence is neither house breaking nor burglary because the element of "breaking" is lacking. See *State v Onwemunlo*[4].

Breaking may be actual or constructive, it is actual breaking when a person breaks any part of a building whether external or internal or opens by unloading, pulling, pushing, lifting or another means whatever, any door, window, shutter, cellar flap, or other thing, intended to do or cover an opening in a building or an opening giving passage from one part of a building to another. Thus there is breaking also when a person opens a door with a key, lifts a latch, or pushes window.

Constructive breaking occurs when entrance into a dwelling house is obtained by means of any threat or artifice used for that purpose, or by collusion with any person in the building, or where entry is made through a climbing or other aperture of the building permanently left

---

[4]   (1967-68) W.S.N.L.R 137.

open for any necessary purpose, but not intended to be ordinarily used as a means of entrance.

ENTRY

There must be entry. It is deemed as entry if any part of the accused body enters the house or any instrument used by him in breaking the house. Thus it was held in *R v Apesi*[5] that it is sufficient entry where in the process of opening a window the accused's hand or finger enters the room. Brown puts it succinctly thus:

> Entry does not require entry of the whole body: it is sufficient if, say, an arm is put through a broken window to take goods from within[6]

In *Maye Rukuba v Commissioner of Police*[7] the evidence was that he was caught with house breaking tool astride the outer wall of a compound, but there was no evidence of what type of compound. It was held *inter alia* that to convict an accused under section 343 of the penal code law of house trespass the prosecution must prove that

---

5   (1961) W.N.L.R 125

6   Brown O, Crime L.R.611 in Ashworth A. Principles of Criminal Law (1991) Clarendon Press Oxford (1991) p. 344

7   (1967) NNLR 114.

he 'entered' a 'building' used as a human dwelling. The expression 'building' would include a compound walled on all sides but if any part of the compound was unwalled and open then the compound could not properly be described as a building.

Furthermore to constitute entry into a building there must be an introduction of some part of the person's body into the building.

And in *Gambo Dan Mamman v Zaria Native Authority*[8]. The appellant had pleaded guilty to clear charge stating full particulars of lurking house trespass by night contrary to section 356 of the Penal Code and he was convicted. On appeal he stated that he was at the compound by appointment to collect the money owed him by complainant, but did not make this defence during the trial. The trial court did not make this defence during the trial. The trial court did not consider the question whether Musa's house constituted a building within section 343 of the Penal Code. The evidence showed that he entered the complaints compound but not any of the separate rooms.

---

[8]   (1967) NNLR 1.

The court held that the complaints compound which would consist of a number of rooms enclosing a court yard separated from the road by a door or gate is a building within a meaning of section 343 of the Penal Code.

In cases of burglary, in order to enter both the breaking and entry must be at night. If the breaking is in the day time and the entry is at night time or vice versa. The breaking may take place on Wednesday and the entry on Sunday. It is deemed to be burglary provided both of them are done in the night.

It is important to point out that in order to constitute burglary or house breaking and entering with intent to commit a felony. The intent must exist at the time of breaking and entering. Thus in *Uko v The State*[9], the court held that to sustain the charge of breaking and entering under Section 411 of the Criminal Code of the former Eastern Nigeria, it must be proved not only that the accused did not break and enter the complainant's house, but he did so with intent to commit a felony therein.

---

[9]   (1972) NSCC Vol.7 600 at 602.

PUNISHMENT FOR HOUSE BREAKING

In prescrining the punishment for house breaking the Code distinguished ordinary house and house breaking by night. It provides thus:

Section 353

> Whoever commits lurking house trespass or house breaking, shall be punished with imprisonment for a term which may extend to two years and shall also be liable to fine

While Section 355 provided:

> Whoever commits lurking house trespassing by night or house breaking by night, shall be punished with imprisonment for a term which may extend to three years and shall also be liable to a fine[10].

---

[10] The section was amended in 1969 to increase the penalty to "not less than five years and not less than twelve strokes of the cane, with or without a fine" by edict No. 5 1969.

Where however the offence of house breaking is committed in order to commit an offence punishable with imprisonment a more severe penalty of fourteen years and a fine is prescribed[11]. While a life term imprisonment is provided for the offence of house breaking by night to commit an offence punishable with imprisonment[12].

---

[11] Section 354 of the Penal Code Law cap 89 Laws of Northern Nigeria. The section was amended in 1969 to increase the penalty to "not less than 21 years and not less than twelve strokes of the cane, with or without a fine" by edict No.5 1969.

[12] Section 356 of the Penal Code Law cap 89 Laws of Northern Nigeria. The section was amended in 1969 to increase the penalty to "not less than fourteen years and not less than twelve strokes of the cane, with or without a fine" by edict No.5 1969

CHAPTER V

Major Crime Statistics In Adamawa, Borno, Taraba And Yobe States

The crimes of armed robbery, theft and house breaking share a common denominator and that is they all touch on the lives, privacy, properties and liberty of individuals. We have seen that the 1999 constitution of the Federal Republic of Nigeria guarantees these rights. The consequences of these crimes are that individuals may loose their lives, properties and liberties. In some cases the victims become incapacitated by reasons of the injuries inflicted on them by these criminals.

The police plays a vital role in the administration of criminal justice. It is the police that makes the arrest[1] of the suspects and

---

[1]   See Chapter V

consequently reported cases of crimes must first come from them for possible prosecution. The police in Nigeria today is ill funded, they are ill equipped. In most situations the police are being killed by criminals because these criminals are armed with more sophisticated weapons. The Government should provide the necessary equipment for them to effectively combat crime. The welfare package of the police should be enhanced in order to provide a conducive atmosphere for the police to work more efficiently. It is common knowledge that the North East sub-region is facing serious crime waves especially armed robbery. The government s of Borno, Yobe, Taraba and Adamawa States should put heads together in this regard by providing necessary assistance to the police in order for them to be more effective. This will go a long way in checking the rate of commission of these crimes and this will mean that societies will be safe. In this way these fundamental rights as guaranteed would be more meaningful.

It would be preposterous not to acknowledge the efforts of the police in these states bearing in mind the inadequacy of both logistic support and personnel. It not in doubt that the area covered by these states is not only extensive but is bordered by a number of countries where conflict situations exist. Hence in looking at the statistics below one must bear in mind the inadequacies of the police to fully appreciate their performance.

ADAMAWA STATE[2]

Armed Robbery

Over the years under review, armed robbery growth rate stood at 8.2% per annum with some fluctuations.

Theft

Cases of theft however, show a gradual decline from 1990 up to 1995 at a rate of 14% per annum. There was a negative change in 1996 and 1997 which gives an overall increase of 26%.

House Breaking

House breaking increased at a steady rate of 27% until the sudden increase in 1996 and 1997 which changed the percentage increase to about 41% per annum.

---

[2]   See Appendix I

It is obvious from the above that offences of armed robbery, theft and house breaking in Adamawa state has been on the increase however the rates differ.

BORNO STATE[3]

Armed Robbery

The situation in Borno State is somehow different. The figures show a steady decline of 10% over the years and the trend takes a smooth downward movement.

Theft and House Breaking

Theft and house breaking too are on the decline with a rate of 10% and 20% respectively[4].

The downward movement could be due to the increased security efforts in trying to curb the criminal activities. This does not however mean that the situation is good, given the high figures, much is still required to further reduce the crime rate.

---

[3]   See Appendix II

[4]   Supra.

YOBE STATE[5]

Armed robbery

Here the armed robbery rate has been on steady increase with about 30% per annum. This figure indicates a high level of cases of robbery in the state and also only reflective in terms of reported cases.

Theft and House breaking

These two offences have been on the decrease with the following rates, 7% and 12% respectively. These figures are similar to what is obtained in Borno State[6]. That is declining rate of the criminal activities as well.

TARABA STATE[7]

The overall crime rate in Taraba state has been on the increase with armed robbery, theft and house breaking having the following figures; 22%, 17% and 26% respectively.

---

[5] See Appendix III

[6] See Appendix II and III

[7] See Appendix IV

General Percentage of the Crimes.

State	Armed Robbery	Theft	House Breaking
Adamawa	20.7%	13.1%	22.2%
Borno	32.9%	38.2%	27.7%
Taraba	20.5%	36.0%	44.6%
Yobe	25.9%	12.7%	5.5%

The overall crime activities in the states show that Borno ranks the highest in armed robbery and theft, while Taraba has the highest figure in house breaking. Despite the high figures in Borno, it has a general decreasing rate of 9% per annum. The situation in Taraba is however different with an upward trend at a rate of 19.5% per annum and low initial reported figures.

APPENDICES

APPENDIX I

Major Crime Statistics, Returns: Adamawa State

YEARS	1990	1991	1992	1993	1994	1995	1996	1997
ARMED ROBBERY	12	18	28	30	2	43	50	28
THEFT	120	100	50	58	52	50	952	797
BURGLARY	15	NIL	20	NIL	NIL	125	NIL	NIL
HOUSE BREAKING	14	20	28	40	14	60	238	230
TOTAL	161	138	126	128	68	278	1240	1055

Source: *Adamawa State Police Command*

APPENDIX II

Major Crime Statistics, Returns: Borno State

YEARS	1990	1991	1992	1993	1994	1995	1996	1997
ARMED ROBBERY	82	58	37	21	23	48	36	37
THEFT	1400	867	1285	294	650	509	686	663
BURGLARY	NIL	NIL	20	NIL	NIL	125	NIL	NIL
HOUSE BREAKING	149	115	211	48	73	74	78	63
TOTAL								

Source: *Borno State Police Command*

APPENDIX III

Major Crime Statistics, Returns: Taraba State

YEARS	1990	1991	1992	1993	1994	1995	1996	1997
ARMED ROBBERY	-	5	26	33	35	46	48	22
THEFT	-	164	622	730	820	1017	1134	499
BURGLARY	-	NIL	NIL	NIL	NIL	6	1	NIL
HOUSE BREAKING	-	47	177	231	105	114	376	253
TOTAL								

Source: *Taraba State Police Command*

APPENDIX IV

Major Crime Statistics, Returns: Yobe State

YEARS	1990	1991	1992	1993	1994	1995	1996	1997
ARMED ROBBERY	-	-	19	23	48	45	40	94
THEFT	-	-	462	306	305	376	354	308
BURGLARY	-	-	NIL	NIL	1	NIL	9	1
HOUSE BREAKING	-	-	46	35	10	27	23	22
TOTAL								

Source: *Taraba State Police Command*

BIBLIOGRAPHY

Abramson   Crime and the Human Mind. New York Columbia University Press (1944).

Aduba J.N.   "Recording of Crime in Nigeria: Problem and Prospects" (1992) Jus. Vol.3 Nos.7 and 8.

Ashworth A.   Principles of Criminal Law. Clarendon Press Oxford (1991).

Bowlby J   "Forty-four Juvenile Thieves" International Journal of Psychoanalysis 25.

C.F.L Membere   Standard Police Manual Vol. 1 Police (Nigeria) and Law Enforcement. P.Koda Pubs L.T.D Benin City (1982)

Chukkol K.S.	"The Reasonableman: Does he "exist" under the Penal Code?" (1984) The Nigerian Law Journal 39.
Clark R.	Crime in America, New York, Simon and Schuster (1970).
Conklin J.E	Criminology. 3rd Edition. Macmillan Publishing Company New York. (1986).
Curzon L.B.	Criminal Law 6th Edition. Longman Group U.K. ltd. (1991).
Dambazau	Criminology and Criminal Justice. Nigeria Academy Kaduna 1991.
Durkhein E.	The Division of Labour in Society. (Trans) G. Simpson Glencoe III. Free Press1895, 1933.
Fawhenmi G	Ed. Digest of the Supreme Court Cases 1956-1984.
Glueck S. and Glueck E	Unravelling Juvenile Delinquency (Cambridge, Mass.:Havard University Press 1950).
Hooton E.A.	The American Criminal: An Anthropological Study. Cambridge, Mass: Harvard University Press 1939.

Jeffery C.R.	"An Integrated Theory of Crime and Criminal Behaviour" Journal of Society of Comparative Legislation.
Jones J.R.	Criminal Procedure Code in the Northern States of Nigeria 2nd Ed. Gaskiya Corporation Ltd Zaria. 1987
Mayer S.E.	"The Consequences of Inequality; The State o Current Research" Joint Centre for Poverty Research News, Vol. II No.3 Summer 1998.
Millerson G.	"Criminal Statistics and the Perks Committee" (1968) Crim. L.R 478.
Ofori-Aman Kwa	An Introduction to the Criminal Law of the Northern States of Nigeria (1997).
Okonkwo C.O.	Okonkwo and Naisa on Criminal Law in Nigeria. Spectrum Law Publishong, Ibadan. 1980.
Piaget J	The Moral Judgement of the Child. London, Kegan Paul. 1932
Richard C.	Criminal Law (1992) 12th Edition Butherwoiths, London.

Richardson S.S.   Notes on the Penal Code Law (Cap 89 Laws of Northern Nigeria 3rd Edition. (1963).

Sellin T.   "The Significance of Records of Crime" L.Q.R 489.

Shepherd J.   Sociology, St. Paul Min, West Publishing, 1981.

Slainner B.F.   The Behaviour of Organing, New York; Applenton Centurt Crofts. (1938).

Smith J.C and Hogan B.   Criminal Law. 16th ed. London Butterworths 1988.

Smith J.C and Hogan B.   Criminal Law. 16th ed. London Butterworths 1992.

Sutherland E.H.   Principles of Criminology. Philadelphia; Lippincott.

Taylor L.   Born to Crime: The Genetic Causes of Criminal Behaviour. London Coteen Wood Press (1984)

DR. MARYAM ISHAKU GWANGNDI
& SULE MUSA TAGI

The Authors are lecturers in the Department of Public Law, University of Maiduguri. They have also been engaged in active Law practice. Their combined efforts has brought out the Law relating to Armed Robbery, Theft and House Breaking in Nigeria with particular emphasis on the commission of these crimes in Adamawa, Borno, Taraba and Yobe States. They have also endeavoured to highlight the relevance of criminal statistics.

INDEX

A

A.B. Dambazau   9, 11, 14, 17-18

Abettor   45-6

Abject neglect   20

Accountancy week   3

Acholono, JCA   29

Actus reus   10, 34-5

Adamawa State   55-6, 59

Adeyemi v The State   30

Administrators   6, 8

Adult Offender   16

Ajao v State   25

Alasho Anaho and Anor v Keffi N.A.   39

Allen   14

Allen, C.K.   14

American Criminal   15, 64

Anarchy   3

Anita Pollock   16

Annual reports   7

A.O.P. Okumu   3

Apathy   18

Apprehension   29

Armed bandits   21

Armed Robbery   iii, vii-ix, xv, xix, 3-5, 7, 9, 11, 13-15, 17, 19-23, 25-9, 31-2, 35, 53-62

Armed Robbery Tribunal   31-2

Arrest   viii, 53

Ashworth A.   48, 63

Audu Pankshin   37

B

Babalola and Anor v The State   30

barrelled weapon   32

Benin City   7, 63

Biogenetic factors   15

Black's Law Dictionary   22, 33, 43

Borders   20

Borno State   x, xxi, 56-7, 60

Borth—Y—GEST   28

Bozin v The State   26

British Academy   14

Brown   48

Brown O   48

Bullet   32

Burglary   4, 7, 14, 19, 25, 43-4, 46-7, 50, 59-62

Butterworths   10, 66

C

Cambridge   15, 64

Chief Magistrate   38

Child poverty   17

Clark   17, 38, 64

Clark R.   17, 64

Commission   vii-ix, 4, 19, 21, 25, 27, 44, 54, 67

Conklin J.E.   10

Constitution   1-2, 4-5, 53

constitutional rights   19

Constructive breaking   47

Corruption   16

Court of Appeal   xxi, 26, 32, 36

Crime   1, 5-7, 9-18, 21, 27, 29, 43, 48, 53-4, 56-66

Crime in America   17, 64

Crime in Nigeria   7, 63

Criminal Act   17

Criminal behaviour   11-12, 15-16,

   18-19, 65-6

Criminal code   38, 50

Criminal justice   ix-x, 9, 21, 53, 64

Criminal Law   10-11, 13-14, 25,

   35, 39, 48, 63-6

Criminal misappropriation   35

Criminal procedure   13, 65

Criminal procedure code   65

Criminal statistics   viii, 1, 5-9,

   65, 67

Criminal tendencies   15, 19

Criminologist   11

Criminology   9-10, 12, 16, 18,

   64, 66

Criminology and criminal justice

   9, 64

Criminology and Police science   12

Cultural values   10

Culture   11

Custody   38, 40

D

D.Abramen   16

Decree   31-2

Decree, No.47   31

Decree No. 21   31

Decree No.5   31

Decree No.62   32

Democratic society   5

Denning J.   28

Dennis James v C.O.P   38

Dermot Walse   18

Digest of the Supreme Court Cases

   25, 30, 64

Drug abuse   16-17

Durkheim   16

E

E. Glueck   16

East Africa   xxi

Eastern Nigeria   50

E.Durkheim   16

English Common Law   27

Entry   47-50

Environment   16-18

environmental designs   16

Ethical   9

European parliament   16-17

Evidence Act   27

Extortion   23-4

F

Factors   viii, 1, 11-12, 15-16, 18

Federal Republic   1-2, 5, 53

Federal Republic of Nigeria   1-2, 5, 53

Federation of Nigeria   27

Felonious   23

Figbene membere   6

Firearms   25, 31

Fraud   14

Fundamental human right   1

Fundamental rights   5, 54

G

G. Simpson   64

Gambo Dan Mamman v Zaria Native Authority   49

genetic mutation and heredity   15

Geoffrey Millerson   7

Globalisation   10

God   29

Guilty Act   10

H

High court   32

High technology   16

Hogan B.   39, 66

Hooton E.   64

House of Lords   27, 36

Housebreakers   8, 21

Housebreaking   14, 19

Human right   1

I

Ideological Orientation   9

Ikemson v State   25-6

Imprisonment   10, 31-2, 40-2, 44,
   51-2

International Journal of
   Psychoanalysis   16, 63

Intimidation   29

J

J. Piaget   16

J.Bowlby   16

Jeffery C.R.   65

Journal of Contemporary legal
   problems   7

Judges   3, 13

Jurisdiction   1, 31-2

Juvenile Delinquency   16, 64

Juvenile thieves   16, 63

K

Kaduna   9, 64

Kegan Paul   65

L

Laboratory   38

Law   vii-ix, xi-xii, xxi, 3-5, 7-11,
   13-15, 21-3, 25, 27, 35, 37,
   39-45, 47-9, 51-2, 63-7

Law enforcement   viii, 7, 63

Law Quarterly Review   8

Laws of Northern Nigeria   23,
   52, 66

Laws of the Federation   27

Legal prohibition   9

Legal System   13

Legislators   6, 8

Local thieves   21

London   10, 15-17, 25, 35-6,
   39, 65-6

Lord Delvin 14

Lord Moris 28

Lower Court 37

M

The Maccabean Lecture 14

Maiduguri xii, 3, 67

Mala prohibitum 11

Mancini v D.P.P 27

Martins v The State 26

Maximum punishment 42

Maye Rukuba v Commisioner of

   Police 41

Mens rea 10-11, 38-9

Mental element 10, 38

Mental stress 18

Microscope 38

Military Government 41

Miller v Minister of Pensions 28

N

N. Aduba 7

New Scotland Yard 17

New York 2, 10, 12, 16-17, 63-4, 66

Nigeria iii, ix, xii, xv, xix, xxi,

   1-3, 5-7, 9, 11, 13, 23, 27,

   49-55, 63-7

Nigerian Constitution 4

Nigerian Defence Academy 9

Nigerian Government 5, 19

Nigerian Laws 4

Nigerian Police Force 6

Nigerian society 1, 3, 13, 15-16

Njuguma v R 25

Norms 11

North East sub-region 7, 54

North Eastern State 41

Nwomukoro and ORS v

   The State 29

O

Offence of robbery   24-6, 31-2

Offence of theft   34, 37, 39, 42

Offender   16, 23-4, 31-2

Offensive weapon   25, 31

Okobi v State   30

Organisation of African Unity   2

Otti v State   25

P

Paul Condon   17

Penal code   vii, 4, 23, 31-2, 34-5,
    38-41, 44, 46, 48-50, 52, 64, 66

Penal treatment   8

Penalty   vii, 41-2, 51-2

Personality disorders   16

Philadelphia   16, 66

Physical violence   14

Police   xi, 5-8, 12, 20-1, 41, 48,
    53-5, 59-63

Policeman   21

Political ideology   1

Poor   16-18

Poor education   16

Professor Thorsten Sellin   8

Property rights   14

Protective laws   1

Public Health   5

Public Morality   5, 13

Public Order   5

Public Safety   5

Punishment   10, 31, 39-40, 42,
    44, 51

R

R v Apesi   48

R v Bekun   24

R v Desmond   28

R v Fallow   30

R v Hall   28

R v Lawrence   27, 36

Rebels   20

Records of crimes   8

Rich   17-18

Richard   25, 65

Robbery   iii, vii-ix, xv, xix, 3-5, 7,

9, 11, 13-15, 17, 19-32, 35, 37,

39, 53-62

Royakiga   37

S

S. Glueck   16

Security   1, 3, 7, 14, 19, 56

Smith and Hogan   13

Smith J.C   35, 39, 66

Social and environmental   16

Social Stress   17

Standard Police Manual   7, 63

T

Taraba State   57, 61-2

Taylor   15, 36, 66

Teacher Training College   38

Terrorism   3

Theft   iii, vii-ix, xv, xix, 3-5, 7,

9, 11, 13-15, 17, 19, 21, 23-5,

33-42, 55-62

U

Uko v The State   50

Unemployment   16-19

United Nations Research Institute   9

Universal Declaration of Human

Rights   2, 4-5

Urban degradation   17

Urbanisation   16

W

Welfare   1, 19, 54

Woolmington v D.P.P   27

Y

Yobe State   57, 62